The Smart & Easy Guide To Debt Relief: How to Live Debt Free with These Credit Score Repair Tips, Debt Repair Advice, Debt Settlement Management & Credit Counseling Help

Darryl Johnson

Legal Stuff

Copyright Information

Copyright © 2013 Checkmate Marketing Group LLC. All rights reserved worldwide.

No part of this publication may be replicated, redistributed, or given away in any form without the prior written consent of the publisher.

Checkmate Marketing Group LLC

Earnings Disclaimer

EVERY EFFORT HAS BEEN MADE TO ACCURATELY REPRESENT THIS PRODUCT AND IT'S POTENTIAL. IN TERMS OF EARNINGS, THERE IS NO GUARANTEE THAT YOU WILL EARN ANY MONEY USING THE TECHNIQUES AND IDEAS IN THIS MATERIAL. INFORMATION PRESENTED ON THIS BOOK IS NOT TO BE INTERPRETED AS A PROMISE OR GUARANTEE OF EARNINGS. EARNING POTENTIAL IS ENTIRELY DEPENDENT ON THE PERSON USING OUR PRODUCT, IDEAS AND TECHNIQUES.

ANY CLAIMS MADE OF ACTUAL EARNINGS OR EXAMPLES OF ACTUAL RESULTS CAN BE VERIFIED UPON REQUEST. YOUR LEVEL OF SUCCESS IN ATTAINING THE RESULTS CLAIMED IN OUR MATERIALS DEPENDS ON THE TIME YOU DEVOTE TO THE PROGRAM, IDEAS AND TECHNIQUES MENTIONED, YOUR FINANCES, KNOWLEDGE AND VARIOUS SKILLS. SINCE THESE FACTORS DIFFER ACCORDING TO INDIVIDUALS, WE CANNOT GUARANTEE YOUR SUCCESS OR INCOME LEVEL.

ANY AND ALL FORWARD LOOKING STATEMENTS HERE OR ON ANY OF OUR SALES MATERIAL ARE INTENDED TO EXPRESS OUR OPINION OF EARNINGS POTENTIAL. MANY FACTORS WILL BE IMPORTANT IN DETERMINING YOUR ACTUAL RESULTS AND NO GUARANTEES ARE MADE THAT YOU WILL ACHIEVE RESULTS SIMILAR TO OURS OR ANYONE ELSES. NO GUARANTEES ARE MADE THAT YOU WILL ACHIEVE ANY RESULTS FROM OUR IDEAS AND TECHNIQUES IN OUR MATERIAL.

Limitation of Liability

THE MATERIALS IN THIS BOOK ARE PROVIDED "AS IS" WITHOUT ANY EXPRESS OR IMPLIED WARRANTY OF ANY KIND INCLUDING WARRANTIES OF MERCHANTABILITY, NONINFRINGEMENT OF INTELLECTUAL PROPERTY, OR FITNESS FOR ANY PARTICULAR PURPOSE. IN NO EVENT SHALL OR ITS AGENTS OR OFFICERS BE LIABLE FOR ANY DAMAGES WHATSOEVER (INCLUDING, WITHOUT LIMITATION, DAMAGES FOR LOSS OF PROFITS, BUSINESS INTERRUPTION, LOSS OF INFORMATION, INJURY OR DEATH) ARISING OUT OF THE USE OF OR INABILITY TO USE THE MATERIALS, EVEN IF HAS BEEN ADVISED OF THE POSSIBILITY OF SUCH LOSS OR DAMAGES.

Table of Contents

Introduction 6
Getting Started 9
A Guide to Credit 12
Understanding Home Mortgages 19
A Step By Step Guide to Get Out of Debt 23
Options: Debt Settlement and Credit Counseling 39
Changing your Attitude Towards Money 44
We Want Your Feedback on This Book! 49

Introduction

Within the current economy it seems that most people are not equipped to deal with money and due to this many of these people miss out on refinancing their homes, or even qualifying for loans that could get them a new vehicle. There are several things that most people think of as basic knowledge when it comes to the credit the person has, such as paying your bills on time, not having a lot of credit card debt and the like. However, this basic knowledge seems to be overlooked by many people throughout the US.

Consider these two scenarios, that seem to be more typical each day in the US:

1. Tom and Maria need to refinance their home loan in order to get a lower payment. Both worked two jobs each, have four kids and many credit cards that are almost maxed to their limit. However, due to their financial situation they do not qualify for any of the refinancing options on the market.

2. Jack and Lisa wanted to purchase a house that is listed for $400,000. Their combined income is $56,000 a year, they both have new cars that they are paying around $1200 a month for, and they have around $30,000 in credit card debt. The monthly amount they would pay for such a house would be around $3,450.

In both of these situations what is holding these couples back is their credit score. They do not have the score that loan companies deem as appropriate to lend to. Or if they do get a company who will give them the money, they are paying astronomical rates for this. What is wrong with these situations is that people are not taking credit seriously. The main reason that comes to most people's mind in the financial district is that people really do not understand what credit is in terms of how this will affect the person. We live in an economy in which we are bombarded with ideas of buying the next greatest thing, and many of these ads are catered towards kids. Thus, kids are growing up thinking that they have to have the best of everything or they cannot live without the latest gadget. Most kids look at money as being a plastic card rather than green dollars. But consider this, how many times do you see advertisements or commercials geared towards saving money? There aren't many, because that is not how this society works.

Aside from being constantly driven to buy more, we are not taught about credit. We don't know how it works. And most companies that deal with credit would prefer that people do not know since it means these companies are earning more money. These types of companies only make a profit when a person is in debt. Once you understand how great works, you are going to find that you will never look at credit in the same way, in fact you may be shocked at what you learn.

Right now is the time to take action if you are swimming in debt and believe that your credit is being affected, which it is. You cannot rely on someone else to help with this, as this is a personal decision. This book is going to teach you all that you need to know in order to get out of debt. Yet, this book is different than others on the market, simply because you are also being taught the fundamentals of credit and how to ensure that you do not find yourself in this situation again. The whole idea around credit is to learn how to better manage the money you make, without having to rely on credit cards. The goal of this book is to make you realize that you must take a stand and take charge of your credit, otherwise it will eventually swallow you up.

Getting Started

There are many different ways in which a person can get out of debt, and which one who choose is going to depend on your particular situation. All of these approaches are identified below to help you gain a better understanding of what you could do, and then choose the best choice based off of what situation you find yourself in.

For those who have been paying their bills on time, who have a good credit rating and need to find a way to get out of debt in order to keep their good credit, then they are going to find that their best chance is to follow the advice found in "A Step by Step Guide to Get out of Debt". They will find that other options will not work for them at all.

If you find that your are past due on account and you simply cannot afford to make the payments, then credit counseling or debt settlement is going to be the best choice for you. This information can be found in "Options: Debt Settlement and Credit Counseling".

For every situation a person may have, they are going to find that there is a different way to proceed when it comes to dealing with their credit. There is no solution that is going to be a one size fits all sort of solution. However, you should keep in ind that money problems that most people have are a result of how they think, rather than it simply being a financial problem. This may sound a bit far fetched, but consider this example. If a self made millionaire were to have all their money taken away, would this person sit there and whine about it being taken away or would they simply make more? This type of person would simply make more because they have a different view on money than what the rest of the world does. When you take this example compared to the number of lottery winners who have blown all their money rather than make this money earn more money for them, it shows that the attitudes of people need to change in order to effectively deal with debt.

Luck is a concept that many people use in the financial world, yet really is there such a thing as luck? We have control over our lives and we can change our destiny with ease. This is a concept that is touched on in "Changing your Attitude Towards Money", and it is one section that everyone must read in order to get a better understanding of their own finances. Even those who may not be in debt right now, may still be forced into this situation when they get older.

From an early age we are taught that things are limited, limited money, limited jobs, and so forth. We have had this drilled into our heads so much so that we fail to see the world around us. We all become obsessed with money at one point in our lives, however, we must get passed this in order to live our lives fully. The first step is to get yourself out of debt as this is going to help you to become more independent and less dependent upon whatever the credit card companies and loan companies want. When you have a good credit score you will find that this affects everything in your life, including the house you get and the medical insurance you qualify for.

For those who are ready to start their lives being debt free, then they need to begin with the section, "A Guide to Credit", and from there they can find out what they need to know in order to ensure their lives are free from debt and they are getting the most out of their financial life.

A Guide to Credit

Most people will find that the majority of their debt is from credit cards. These are rather easy for anyone to gain access to, yet most people do not realize how these credit cards work. The credit system in general, is going to work against you unless you know what you are doing and are prepared for what is being thrown your way. You will need to know how credit really works, what compound interest is and how this works, once you do you an start to use credit to help you rather than being a victim of this.

Here are a few facts that you may find interesting and puts the whole credit concept into perspective:

1. There were six billion credit card offers sent out in the email during 2005, all of which had the person as being pre-approved.
2. In 1995, only 2.7 billion offers for pre-approved credit cards were mailed out.
3. All of these types of offers received in the mail have a great introductory rate, but after a few months the rate usually doubles. Consider this offer below that was given to a consumer from Chase Bank, be sure that you are looking at the fine print that is being seen:

"Rates, Fees and terms may change: We reserve the right to change the terms of your account (including the APRs) at any time, for any reason, in addition to APR increases that may occur for failure to comply with the terms of your account".

Note the idea, that the bank can change this for any time and for any reason, and of course when you fail to pay on time or the like. What this shows is that the deal you think you are getting is not as great as you think it is. The banks have complete control when they issue a credit card like this to you. And you cannot beat the bank when it comes to this. They write these rules with their bank in mind, they are not out there to ensure that their customers well being is being taken into consideration. In addition, there are billions of dollars spent each year by these companies that are lobbying for laws that are going to be passed by Congree which benefit them and not you. With all this being said, you have no hope if you want to go up against these companies.

There is some good news in spite of what a person may be thinking at this point, you do not have to beat the companies at their game, you simply have to understand it and this means having a good knowledge of how credit works. First off, the person needs to remember that just because you get a pre-approved letter does not mean that you are going to get approved for the credit card at all. These companies pay for a list of people who have used credit cards in the past from the major credit bureaus, and they simply send these out hoping that someone is going to take the offer. If you want these offers to stop coming in the mail because they may be too tempting or you are simply tired of receiving these then you can call (888) 567-8688 which will get you in contact with the Credit Bureaus and you can be taken off of their pre-approved lists. Keep in mind that if you do opt out for these offers that you can greatly decrease your chances of identity theft. If you would rather talk to each bureau individually, then you can use the following addresses and phone numbers and simply tell them you want to opt-out of pre-approval lists:

Equifax: PO Box 7401243 Atlanta, GA 30374-0123; (800) 556-4711

Experian Consumer Opt Out: 701 Experian Parkway Allen TX, 75013; (800) 353-0809

TransUnion Attn Marketing Opt Out: PO Box 97328 Jackson MS, 39288-7328; (800) 680-7293

One term that has become popular in the last few years in terms of credit, is the term 'Grace Period'. This is the number of days you have to pay on something before the balance is subjected to the interest that the company is going to charge. The time frame used to be thirty days, yet more and more cards are on a 21 day grace period. This does mean that you have less time to pay your card in full and that the company is likely to get more money since they can charge interest earlier. The interest that is charged on a credit card is from the date of purchase, meaning if you have paid half of this off, you are still getting interest charged to you as though it was the full amount, this is something that many people are surprised to learn.

Another term to look out for is the 'over the limit fee'. Most people think that if they use their card and they do not have the funds that the transaction would be denied. However, many credit card companies are allowing a person to go over their limit and then slap them with a fee that can be as little as twenty dollars or as much as fifty dollars. And on top of this, the price of late fees have increased from a mere ten dollars to over fifty dollars for some people. In addition to these factors, when a person makes a payment late or they go over their limit, their interest rate usually increases. An example, someone who sent their payment in late had their interest rate jump from nine percent to 29%. This is a common scenario that people need to be aware of.

Another aspect that most people do not think about, and this is not going to apply to everyone is the Foreign Transaction fee that companies charge a person if there were to withdraw money from an ATM that is located outside of the US. This is something that you need to remember if you plan on using a card while traveling. In addition, you will be hit with two fees when withdrawing money from a bank. The ATM will charge a fee, and then the company will charge a fee for the money being withdrawn from an ATM that does not belong to them. You could end up paying around six dollars in fees just for withdrawing money.

These are just a few fees that a person has to be aware of, as there are really too many to even make a list. So most people are asking themselves at this point what they can do in order to protect themselves?

The first thing you need to do is look over your statement each month, most people do not check their statement they simply send their payment and go on. You will also need to look at your banking statements. You will want to look for anything that may be an error, including to see if any fees that have been applied are correct. If you do see late fees or fees for being over your limit, you can ask for the company to waive them. If this is the first time that you have even been late or went over your limit, many companies will give you another chance. However, only expect for this to work once.

You will want to ensure that you are giving your payment at least ten days to get to where it needs to be. This is going to help you to avoid late fees. You can also set up this payment to be deducted automatically from your checking account if you want to ensure you never have to worry about late fees and penalties.

Most importantly, be sure that you call your companies and ask them to reduce your interest rate. Though many people do not think of this, most companies are willing to do this. However, if you don't succeed at first, keep calling every week and see if you do not finally wear them down.

Understanding Compound Interest

If you truly want to stay out of debt, there is no other term more important than understanding than compound interest. In order to understand this concept, consider this question: If you could choose between getting on million dollars today, or choosing to receive one penny a day, two pennies the next, four pennies the next, eight pennies the next and so forth for the following thirty days? Which would you choose? Most people would go with the million dollars, and this is a good choice. But, look at the penny method, which is how compound interest works. The list below shows just how compound interest can accumulate:

Day 1: $.01
Day 2: $.02
Day 3: $.04
Day 4: $.08
Day 5: $.16
Day 6: $.32
Day 7: $.64
Day 8: $1.28
Day 9: $2.56
Day 10: $5.12
Day 11: $10.24
Day 12: $20.48
Day 13: $40.96
Day 14: $81.92
Day 15: $163.84
Day 16: $327.68
Day 17: $655.36

Day 18: $1,310.72
Day 19: $2,621.44
Day 20: $5,242.88
Day 21: $10,485.76
Day 22: $20,971.52
Day 23: $41,943.04
Day 24: $83,386.08
Day 25: $167,772.16
Day 26: $335,544.32
Day 27: $671,088.64
Day 28: $1,342,177.28
Day 29: $2,684,354.56
Day 30: $5,368,709.12

This just goes to show that compound interest is something that can accumulate to large sums in just a small amount of time. Einstein often said that compound interest was the most powerful source that is in the universe, and it would seem that he war correct. With the table above we see that in 30 days, a person would get over $5,000,000. This is the type of formula that credit card companies are using. When you have a credit card you pay interest on the balance you have, but you are also paying interest on the interest that you have had from prior months.

If you are only making a minimum payment on your card, you are going to find that this compound interest is seriously hurting you. This type of interest is calculated daily, meaning that any balance you have is subjected to this each day. Every time that you pay the minimum, you are putting more money into the pockets of the credit card company.

A good example for those who are struggling with this concept is a credit card with a balance of $5,000 at an interest rate of 18%. If you pay the minimum payment of this balance, which is usually only three percent of what you owe, it would take 199 months for you to pay off this card. In interest alone you would have paid almost five thousand dollars, and it would have taken you over sixteen years to pay this. Banks and credit card companies do not want the consumer to know this, since they can make huge profits from people only paying the minimum payment.

Understanding Home Mortgages

It is difficult for many people to think of a home mortgage as being debt, but it is. Even if you claim to own your home. With this being said, if you want to be out of debt, you have to realize how these types of loans are working. Mortgages are basically like credit cards on a larger scale when it comes to how much a person is getting.

Those companies that provide mortgages never state that they compound interest daily, unless this is in the fine print of the thousands of documents you sign when getting a home, but most of these companies do this. Since you realize what compound interest can do, it makes sense to pay off the mortgage you have as soon as possible. Most people are under the assumption that when they get a mortgage with a 6% interest rate, that they are only paying 6% on the total that they borrow.

This only works if you pay off your mortgage in one year. Most people opt for a 30 year mortgage, meaning that you pay around 100% interest on your loan. The table below shows a typical scenario of what you would end up paying with a $200,000 mortgage.

Loan Amount	Interest Rate	Term / Type	Monthly Payment	Total Paid (Principal + Interest)	Interest Paid
$200,000	6%	30 years, fixed	$1199.10	$431,676.80	$231,676.38

The lower the interest rate on the loan, the lower the compound interest. The compound interest is going to be the same as the interest rate you have on the loan. For those who were to get a $300,000 mortgage with a 9.8% rate, they would pay around $631,000 in interest over the course of 30 years.

This can be overwhelming for someone who just got a home and did not know this about their mortgage, yet there are many mortgages out there that have even scarier outcomes. The 'Interest Only' loan is one of those situations. The person is paying on the interest alone, and deferring the total loan amount. However, they are still accumulating interest on the amount they have deferred. You are not paying down the balance of a loan, but you are increasing the total amount of interest that you pay in the end. If you have the idea of selling your home in a few months, this is a loan that could be of interest, but only if the value of the home is going to increase. But, in a market that is being seen around the world right now, this is a huge financial disaster. The only way this is a good choice for someone who intends to stay in the home long term is if they are still paying on the principle and have an incredibly low interest rate.

Another mortgage option is the 'Adjustable Rate Mortgage". Every month the person is given four options as to what they can pay. This is only good for people who have a fluctuating income each month, but for most people out there, this is not the way they want to go. With the first payment option you send less money that what is the interest accumulated this month. For example, a $200,000 mortgage with a rate of 7.683% and a minimum payment of 1.25%, would mean that while you pay around $666, you are deferring $614 that will be added to the balance and will start to collect interest.

The second payment option is that you only pay the interest that has accumulated for that month. With the above example, it would mean that you pay around $1280 for the month, but you are not paying anything on the principal balance.

The third payment option is a regular payment of the principal and interest which would be $1423 for this example. The fourth option allows you to pay the regular payment that is calculated on a 15 year mortgage instead of the standard 30 year mortgage, which would mean paying around $1874.

Which option do you think most people choose? Option one and this is because most companies are sending their statements to consumers with the first option highlighted. Why? Simply because those who pay like this are going to pay more money and they will be paying for much longer than someone who has gotten a typical mortgage loan. It is easy for a person to add $50,000 to a loan and not even realize that this is happening. And the reason for this is that people are not really informed of what they are getting themselves into with this type of mortgage.

There are many people who believe that they should not pay off their mortgage immediately, and they always offer two separate arguments. The first is that the mortgage on a home is giving them tax benefits since you can deduct the interest you pay on your mortgage from your taxes. The second is that the interest rates on their mortgages is low, thus why should they really be concerned about paying this off early.

Looking at both of these arguments, when you get some tax benefit from paying interest on your mortgage, you are only getting back a small amount. For example, you could pay around $10,000 in interest, and at the end of year get back $2500. Why would you want to get back only a small percentage of this when you could pay of the mortgage and have the full $10,000 still? You could take the money you save and put this into an investment for later in life. Though investments are risky, even if you don't do this, you are saving yourself $10,000. As far as the interest rate being low on these loans, even if you pay a small interest rate and only pay around $5000 a year in interest, this is $5000 you could keep in your bank.

In the next section, a person will learn how they can get rid of their debt without declaring bankruptcy, refinancing their home, using debt consolidation or the like. It is a simple plan that anyone can follow with any amount of debt and get their life back on track.

A Step By Step Guide to Get Out of Debt

For those who have made the decision to become debt free, the following steps have been proven to help people become free of debt in a way that is going to make sense, and it is going to allow the person to get out of the debt they have much faster than they would otherwise do this.

The first step is to be committed to getting out of debt and ready to follow the steps to make this happen, and you are going to have to make sure that you follow the plan no matter what you may find out along the way. There are going to be obstacles that may make you feel as though you cannot get out of debt, but you have to take these obstacles and run with them. You will not get out of debt if you are not one hundred percent committed to this program. It may be helpful if you have someone that you can talk to that is going through these steps with you, or who has been in this place before. Having someone that can encourage you along the way is going to make the process emotionally easier. Consider this to be the equivalent of a dieting plan, if there is a support system in place, a person is going to lose more weight than if they were to go at this alone. The same can be said of having some type of support when going through the process of getting out of debt.

The second step is to stop using your credit cards immediately. This is the main step that you need to think about once you have made the commitment. The best plan of attack is to cut up your credit cards so that they are not tempting you to use them, however, you may want to keep a card for an emergency and have this at home, not in your wallet, so you have to make a conscious effort to carry this with you if you need it. This is a habit that is going to be hard to break, yet it is essential to your success to get out debt. You need to remember that from now on if you cannot pay for something with cash, then you cannot buy it, and you really do not need it.

Step three involves finding out just what you are spending your money on. You need to know just what you are buying and how this adds up each month. There are many programs such as Quicken, AceMoney (which is free) and other similar programs that are going to allow you to track your money easily online. If you do not want to do this, then write down everything you spend and have a calculator handy to calculate just what you are spending. You need to write down everything that you are spending, including those things that you buy with cash. Have a small notebook on you at all times so you can write down everything that is paid for with cash. The following is an example of what could be someone's daily record:

Thursday, February 15

Coffee & pastry	$3.50
Lunch	$7.90
Magazine	$5.00
Soda	$1.00
Vending machine	$1.00
Groceries	$76.85

Now when you wonder just what did you spend that twenty dollar bill on, you will have it written down and can find out exactly what you did with your money. If you start to track down your expenses, you will start to notice whether you are throwing away money on things that you can live without. The following is an example of a weekly record:

February 8-14

Breakfast	$17.50
Lunch	$42.00
Office Depot	$25.00
Entertainment	$14.00
Snacks	$12.00
Groceries	$126.85
Gasoline	$41.00

You have taken all of your daily logs and put them into a weekly format to have a better idea of just where you are spending each week. Now you will want to take these weeks and put this into a month spending calendar, such as this example:

Spending Record - February

	week 1	week 2	week 3	week 4	TOTAL
Rent / Mortgage	1200				
Groceries	140	87	95	120	442
Lunch	42	46	53	30	171
Breakfast	17.5	22	16	18	34
Laundry	6	6	6	6	16
Gasoline	60	45	70	40	215
Gas & Electric	80	0	0	0	80
Entertainment	30	0	45	15	90
Cell Phone bill	0	0	80	0	80
Cable TV	76	0	0	0	76
Magazines	5	0	0	5	10
Newspaper	2	1.5	2	2	7.5
Office Depot	25	0	0	0	25
Fast Food	22	0	16	26	64
Pizza	12	12	0	0	24

Now that you know where you are spending your money, you need to look for areas in which you can lose or at least trim down a bit. There are many common areas that people will find can be trimmed down, such as:

- If a person eats out at eight dollars per day, they will spend $200 a month on this, and this is figuring low. If you were to take your lunch with you to work a few times a week, you can drastically cut down on what you are spending.

- Getting a coffee a few times per week can amount to up to fifty dollars per month. Instead, make your own coffee from home and only get coffee out as a special treat.

- You cable/satellite may be one hundred dollars per month, however, if you can eliminate some of those channels you do not watch and drop your package, you could cut this down to fifty dollars per month.

- Even if you only eat fast food once a week, you can easily spend one hundred dollars a month. Thus, eat at home as much as you can and leave fast food when you absolutely have to do this.

- If you have magazines that you seldom read, then cancel your subscription, the same can be said of newspapers and the like.

- Rent a movie and pop a bag of microwave popcorn at home instead of going out to the movies on the weekend.

- Use coupons at the grocery store or buy store brands. You are going to find that you can cut a chunk out of your grocery bill when doing this. And only buy those items that you know that you are going to use, do not be fooled by the sale price that may be attached. If you are not going to use it, then you are wasting your money.

- For clothes look at discount stores or consignment stores, you can still find great quality clothing, yet pay half the price.

- Eliminate all those times you go to vending machines for a soda or snack. You can carry your own from home or just take them out of your diet.

- A frozen pizza can be half the price of ordering one, and you can do this within twenty minutes at home.

- Look at your insurance and find out what you can get from other companies. If you can get it cheaper somewhere else, then switch companies as this is money that you can save and put towards your debt.

Remember to be creative in how you are saving money, there may be something that you can do that is not listed here. Anything that you can do to change your lifestyle is going to help lower your debt faster.

The fourth step involves making a budget. You are going to find that most people spend more time planning a weekend trip than they do looking at their budget, and this is a habit that you want to break. If you have a budget, you are going to more apt to get out of and stay out of debt. The following budget spreadsheet can be a great guide to making one for yourself:

Budget Spreadsheet

Income	
Salary	
Overtime / Bonuses	
Other Income	
Monthly Total	

Expenses	
Rent / Mortgage	
Food / Supermarket	
Utilities	
Electric / Gas	
Water	
Cable	
Internet	
Landline Phone	
Cell Phones	
Misc. Utilities	
Car related	
Car payment 1	
Car payment 2	
Car insurance Total	
Gas	
Car expenses: tires, etc.	
Misc	

Balance	Interest Rate

Credit Cards:	
1	
2	
3	
4	
5	
Alimony	
School Tuition	
Clothing	
Food (eating out)	
Student Loans	
Misc (anything else you may spend money on)	
-	
-	
-	
-	
Total Expenses	

Total Income	
Total Expenses	
Total	

The fifth step is to make a list of all the creditors you have and call these creditors. You will want to ask them to lower your interest rate. This may sound odd, but it has worked for many people and it can work for you as well. Here is a simple script that you can use in order to talk to your creditors, if you are stuck on just where to start:

"Hello, my name is _____. I have been a customer with you since _____ and have been a good customer for all of these years. I have started to receive many offers from companies that are offering a lower interest rate on their cards, and I would like to see if you could lower my rate to match these offers."

From here you could go on to state how you would hate to switch credit card companies but you will since the rate is lower. You may even have to ask to talk to their supervisor in order to get anything done. You may want to take this time to ask them about any fees that have been added to the card and see if they remove these as well, such as yearly fees, late fees or the like. If the company doesn't do this at first, call back again.

In order for this to work, you need to be polite about the entire situation. Yet, you still want to be firm. You need to let the company know that you do mean business. Do not yell at the person as they are not responsible for the rate, more than likely they are someone sitting on a phone in a cramped cubicle just answering calls.

Step six is to open a savings account, if you do not already have one and deposit money into this every month. You have to start building your nest egg in order to feel comfortable about not using credit as much, and it will be great for when you have an emergency and you do not want to rely on your credit cards. In order for this to work you need to treat your deposit as though this is just another bill to pay. If you do this, the account will grow quickly, even if you are only able to put in a few bucks each month. Secondly, never take out money from this account unless you do have an emergency that your regular income is not going to cover. If you do have to withdraw money, make sure that you replace this as soon as possible. You will want to let this grow for several years, and once you are debt free you can use this money to fund an investment or the like. You need to realize that a emergency that uses this money is something that is necessary, such as car repair, a medical emergency or the like. An emergency to dive into your savings does not include buying the perfect birthday gift.

Step seven is to fill out the debt eliminate chart and put this into practice immediately. The chart follows:

Get Out Of Debt Chart

My Power Payment will be _____ Start Date _____

My plan to become debt-free

	1	2	3	4	5	6	7
	Debt	Total Owed	Minimum monthly payment	Column 2 ÷ Column 3	Priority	Power Payment	Months to pay off 2 ÷ 6
1							
2							
3							
4							
5							
6							
7							
8							
9							
	Total					Total	

I will be debt-free in _____ months

This program is focusing on only one account at a time, instead of paying extra on all of your accounts. If you were to do this, you are going to feel as though you are not getting anywhere. Therefore, you will pay the minimum amount on all of your other credit cards until the first account is paid off. This is a vital aspect to remember in order for this program to succeed. When you start to divide your extra income among several accounts, you are really not helping to get out of debt any faster, and it will make you discouraged. The following is a mock chart filled out, and the explanation that follows is going to help you to fill out your own debt chart.

	1	2	3	4	5	6	7
	Debt	Total Owed	Min. monthly payment	Col. 2 ÷ Col. 3	Priority	Power Payment	Months to pay off 2 ÷ 6
1	Mastercard	$3,150	$126	25	5	959+126 = $1085	3
2	Mastercard	$8,200	$328	25	6	1085+328= $1413	6
3	Visa	$2,200	$76	25	4	883+76= $959	2
4	Discover	$800	$32	25	3	851+32= $883	1
5	Dept Store	$630	$26	25	2	825+26= $851	1
6	Car 1	$10,200	$425	24	1	400+425 = $825	12
7	Car 2	$15,000	$480	31	7	1413+480= $1893	8
8	Heloc	$30,000	$350	86	8	1893+350= $2243	14
9	Mortgage	$150,000	$1,079	128	9	2243+1079= $3322	45
	Total	$220,180				Total	92

The power payment for this chart shows the amount of $400. It is recommended that you put at least ten percent of your income towards the power payment in order to see the effects of getting out of debt faster. However, you will have to gear your payment towards what works for you. You will know what you can afford once you have made a budget and followed the previous steps mentioned. The chart presented above, whom we will refer to as Nancy and John from California, who have an income of $70,000. This is where the $400 came from, however, even if you can only afford an extra $100 a month, you can still get out of debt, but remember the higher the Power Payment, the sooner you will get out of debt.

To fill out this chart, follow the steps below:

1. Write in the accounts that you owe money to in the first column.
2. The second column is the current balance owed to the creditor
3. Column three is what your minimum payment is on this balance
4. Column four is the combination of dividing column 2 by column 3. This si going to be the number of months that you can expect to pay off the balance with only paying the minimum payments. This is an important number as this is going to determine just how you should arrange your creditors to be paid. The lowest number in this column from all of your creditors is going to be the first card you attack with the Power Payment.
5. On the column five you are going to want to enter the number of priority for each account, focusing on the card with the lowest balance first.

6. The sixth column is where you enter your Power Payment plus the minimum payment in order to see what your total payment will be. In the above example, Car 2 is being the higher priority with a minimum payment of $425 plus a Power Payment of $400, thus the total payment will be $825. You will notice that the increased payment is going to allow for the car to be pad off in twelve months.

Once you have paid off the first priority, you will then go onto the second priority and continue this until you are debt free. Meanwhile, be sure that you are paying the minimum on the accounts that are not receiving the Power Payment.

In order to help you with making this debt plan work, here are a few things to keep in mind:

1. Put the debt elimination chart in a place that you will see it often
2. Cross out creditors that are paid off once they are this way and put the date into the chart.
3. Celebrate when you pay off a creditor as this will encourage you to continue
4. Give yourself a pat on the back for the progress that you are making to ensure that you are going to feel good about the entire process
5. Getting out of debt is not easy and you may find that in order to make your Power Payment some months you may have to take extreme measures such as selling some things, living without a bit more or the like.
6. Once you pay off cards or major purchases like a car, do not give into the temptation to use the card or to buy a new car.
7. Try to keep at least $2000 in your savings for emergencies
8. Have a daily mantra to say to yourself that is going to help you realize that what you are doing is meaningful and your life will be better for it.

There is a lot of pressure on people to keep up with what other people are doing and what they have. The expression, "Keeping up with the Jones'", has become a rule for many families. This is not how you want to live your life, and if you take control of the debt you have, you will be happier with your life in the future. You deserve to be happy and not living your life with a ton of debt on your shoulders.

Options: Debt Settlement and Credit Counseling

In order to understand these options that you have when it comes to your debt, you need to know what the difference is between credit counseling and debt settlement. A credit counselor does not settle your debts for you. They basically can consolidate the debt that you have into one monthly payment, while also lowering the interest rates that are you paying. They will then put forth a debt management plan that you will pay to them, they will divide the money among your creditors. Most people know this as a debt consolidation plan. When working through a company that is creditable, a person can get their debt into one lower payment, yet they are going to pay a fee to the company which can be anywhere from twenty dollars a month to well over fifty dollars a month. Most of these plans are working on a time frame of five years. The rate that these companies negotiate for is around seven to nine percent, which can be a huge different in interest since many people have interest rate that are more like 23%.

You will be asked to cut up the credit cards that you have and do not use these cards ever again while on the plan, which is a good idea anyways. But, you are not going to be given new credit until you have completed the plan. These types of companies are meant to help you manage your finances, while also offering the education that you need to ensure you do not find yourself in this place again.

The problem with credit counseling is that many of these companies do not really have their consumer in mind when they are making these plans. Instead, they are looking for the best way to make money, whether this is through charging excessive fees or not even getting the person the lowest interest rate that they can get. If you are considering this option you must visit the National Foundation for Credit Counseling website in order to find a credit counselor company that is legitimate and works for the consumer.

A debt settlement is much different from credit counseling. With this option, a creditor is going to write off some of the debt that the person has, when the creditor knows that they are not going to be able to get the total amount paid back to them. The reasoning for this type of settlement is that the company believes it is better to get back something rather than nothing. This is not something that everyone is going to be able to do, and if they do manage this they may find that some companies are not willing to work with them at all. If you are able to convince the company as to why you cannot pay the full amount, then you do have a better chance of reaching some sort of settlement. Also keep in mind that when you do settle a credit card, that this does reflect negatively onto your credit report. This is not the option for a person who is paying their bills on time and has a good credit score, and would like to keep it this way.

Debt settlement is really something that should only be used if you are considering filing for bankruptcy. The process of settling your debt is long and it can be reliant upon many factors that a person may not know until they are into the process. You will want to hire a professional in order to get this completed for you, since you do not want to find out that you really messed up later down the line. A professional has done this before and they are going to work to reach a settlement that is going to be favorable to you. With this being said, you should utilize someone who has a good reputation, and someone that you feel comfortable with using.

However, there are many people who decide that they are going to dive into the debt settlement on their own. For those people, the following guidelines can help you to ensure that you are getting a fair deal:

1. This deal is only going to work if your account is past due. Companies only do this if they believe that this is the only way that they are going to see any money. You are going to find that the time frame of four or five months from the last payment is a good time to approach the company. At around six months, companies send these accounts to collection agencies, which is going to mean that you have lost some of your leverage, since the company is more likely to get a full amount when the collection agencies are handling this.

2. Most settlements are going to be around thirty to seventy percent of the total amount that you owe. There are several factors that will affect just how big of a percentage that a person is paying including the negotiating skills you have and how long it has been since you last sent a payment. You will want to aim for a fifty percent reduction in the total amount to be paid, you can start by offering twenty percent, but more than likely you will be denied.

3. You will want to have everything that you need in front of you before you start talking to the company, including statements, creditor letters, and the like. You will want to write down everything you discuss as well as who you talked to to ensure that there are no problems later.

4. Be nice to whoever you are talking to even if they start getting angry at what you are asking. You are going to want to keep your cool because otherwise you are going to get no where with yelling and cussing at them.

5. If they do make an offer that you like, have them send this to you through the mail. Anything that is not in writing is basically useless.

6. If you find that the person you are talking to is getting you no where and they seem to be rude, then disconnect the call and try again later, or ask to speak to a supervisor. If you are polite, there is no need to feel as though you cannot talk to someone else about the situation.

7. Be sure to have all the fees that have been issued onto the account removed, as this is going to greatly lower the balance that you owe. You should not demand this, but you are going to find that if you are polite about it that most companies are trying to do whatever they can do in order to see a bit of the money that is owed to them.

8. Do not lie to the person who you are talking to since these are professionals who have taken courses on what to ask a person to determine if they really do not have the money to pay. You want to be sincere in the amount that you can pay, as they will know if you are lying or not.

9. Have a goal in mind for what you want to pay. For example, if you owe $10,000, having a goal of $5000, is great. If the company wants $8,000, simply remind them that this is not good for you and that you would be better off to file for bankruptcy. It is this type of kick that most companies need in order to negotiate lower.

10. These companies are going to run your credit report and if they see that you have been paying your other bills on time, you are going to find that it is harder to settle with the company. They are going to believe that you could at least make the minimum payments if you are paying every other creditor that you owe.

11. There are basically four things a person needs to know when they want to settle their debt. These are how to communicate, how to negotiate, document what is said, and follow up on whatever is decided upon.

12. Never ever pay over the phone on a deal that was just made. You want the company to send this in writing in order to make sure that everything is right. You can politely decline to pay over the phone and say that you want this in writing.

13. Also use Certified Mail with return receipt on anything that is sent to the creditor, that way there is no chance of anything saying that something was lost.

Most importantly, remember to be polite as this cannot be emphasized enough, as this is vital to getting any kind of deal from a company. You will find better results if you go with a professional, but it is up to you whether you do this or not. If you do want to do this yourself, be sure to read the tips many times and do your research, and even do a mock run through of what you are going to say, anticipating any and all questions.

Changing your Attitude Towards Money

In order to get out of debt, we now realize that we must change our lifestyles and the attitude that we have towards finances. Consider this question, have you ever wanted something yet found for some odd reason you never get it? Most people have at one point in their lives sabotaged something that really meant a great deal to them. The reason for this reaction is because they have conflicting beliefs, some of which they may not even be aware that they are having. These beliefs are based on our past experiences and what we walked away from these with. It is comparative to two people going on the same roller coast ride, yet one person walking away with a happy memory, while the other person walks away thinking about this negatively. It is all in how we look at the event that has happened in our life. With this being said, we need to deal with the experiences we have had and move on. We should never blame the conditions of society, or someone else for the way that we are. With this being said, our beliefs can foster the way that we deal with everything, including our finances.

From a young age there are certain things that we are told such as: You can't do something, you do not have a chance at something, things will only get worse before they get better, and the like. Right now there are 36 million people in America who are 65 years of age and older. Of this number, around 34 million of these people are considered to be broke and they look to someone else for their financial needs. The US is the richest country in the entire world, yet 95% of the people who call this country home are considered to be poverty. Most of those who are in this bracket would say that their life was shaped by experiences. They would basically blame this problem on everyone else. But, it has been proven that the experiences may shape a person but it is how the person perceives this experiences that is really shaping the person they are going to be.

Financial independence is one of those things that people have to strive to find. However, we are never really taught how we can achieve this. Consider this in high school, kids are not taught about how to invest money, how to handle funds or the like. These types of concepts are not even taught at a college level unless the person is going into this field. It would seem that this type of information would be fundamental in coursework for kids. Most people grow up thinking that money is not easy to come by, that the more money you have the lazier you become because you are too rich and the like. The way in which people perceive money is going to be the downfall for their financial independence. For example, consider these ideas that many people have:

- Bad luck is something that just comes to people, a person is going to be either gifted with good luck or cursed with bad luck.
- If you grow up middle class, you are always going to be middle class because that is how you are destined to be.
- Money is always going to be tight because that is just how it is.

Imagine a kid growing up thinking these things, what type of financial independence is this person going to have? They are more than likely going to work a dead end job, afraid of getting another one due to missing out on the small paycheck they are getting. They are also going to believe that they cannot change the course of their life, yet alone improve their financial life. Even those who think that after hearing this they could still make something of themselves, they got to consider how these things have affected their subconscious.

Kids inherit their beliefs from their parents, including those beliefs about money. Therefore, now you have to choose to believe in things that are going to inspire you to do better. For example:

- Money can come easily
- Money can come effortlessly
- I can be wealthy and have an abundant financial life

The good news is that no matter what you believe today, it can be changed tomorrow if you put your mind to it. For those who are in debt, they need to change their beliefs to ensure that they are going to succeed.

The following is a list of good beliefs that a person should strive to have. For those who are in debt, this is a great time to sit and think about these beliefs.

1. There is a good reason for why everything happens, even if I cannot see what this reason is right now.
2. People are basically good
3. Money is something that can be easy to come by
4. Money is always there in abundance within the Universe
5. There is a solution to every existing problem out there, I simply have to find it
6. Being poor is temporary

You can come up with your own set of beliefs, but these will get you started thinking in the right direction.

In order to change your beliefs, there are several methods that you can use. First, you need to identify a belief, which is usually easy as this is the reason that you give for something. When you can write down five beliefs that you have, no matter what these are. Once these are written down, write down five beliefs that are going to help you get to the goals you have in life. You should not feel as though you are limited in what new beliefs you write down, the sky is the limit on what you write.

Now, you need to write down the first old belief that yo have and create doubt about this belief. When you start to doubt this, you are going to slowly stop believing it. Next, write down the new belief that counteracts this old belief and start to repeat this in your head to replace the told belief. This may sound silly, but this method has been proven to work.

For those who are having a hard time in discounting an old belief, ask yourself:

1. Why is this belief ridiculous?
2. What are some negative things that have become from believing in this?
3. What does it cost you now to believe in this, emotionally, physically, financially?
4. How will this belief affect your future?

You need to write down everything that you are thinking. The idea is to write about your pain in order to ensure that this is so painful that your mind immediately deletes it from your brain. You will want to repeat the process for the new belief and ensure that you are feeling happiness while discussing this, in order to make it stick in your mind.

Another method to use to change your beliefs is to make affirmations to yourself. There has been countless studies done that have shown those who have positive affirmations made tho themselves are going to feel better and be more successful. The best way to start an affirmation is to state how happy you are about a certain thing. For example, I am so happy that I have paid off my Visa card. You will want to repeat this consistently throughout the day, as many people have done this hundreds of times per day. You will also want to say these out loud for the best effect. The reason these work is because of the reptation that your mind simply believes these to be fact.

In order to really change your mindset, focus on what successful people have been doing and mimic this. Success people often:

1. Focus on the positive
2. Focus on what it is that they want to achieve
3. They focus on what they like

You have to be positive in order to see any real difference in your life. Even when things seem as though they can get no worse, always look for the positive of what you are seeing. If you find that you are having negative thoughts, then replace these with positive thoughts. Once you do this, you can change your mindset about anything and start to have the life that you have always wanted to have.

We Want Your Feedback on This Book!

Our main purpose is to make sure that our readers get value from the books we publish and that they have a good experience with all of our products. We are always working to improve our books and other products with every revision and update.

Every piece of feedback makes a difference in this process. And we would appreciate yours as well - whether it is good or bad.

Please take one minute to let us know what you thought by following this link:
http://checkmatemg.com/feedbackdebtrelief

www.ingramcontent.com/pod-product-compliance
Lightning Source LLC
Chambersburg PA
CBHW071828170526
45167CB00003B/1462